I Do This For You

Letters To A Daughter Who Deserves The World

La Tanya K. Brown

I Do This For You: Letters To A Daughter That
Deserves The World by La Tanya Allen

Published by La Tanya Brown

Contributions by Veonne Anderson

ISBN: 979-8-218-00315-9 (print)

Printed in United States

1st Edition

I dedicate this book to my daughter LaTanya. My love for you is unconditionally beyond words. Her compassion, genuine respect, loyalty, love and distinctive professionalism deserves recognition. I salute you. I thank God for gifting me with you.

Why I Do This For You

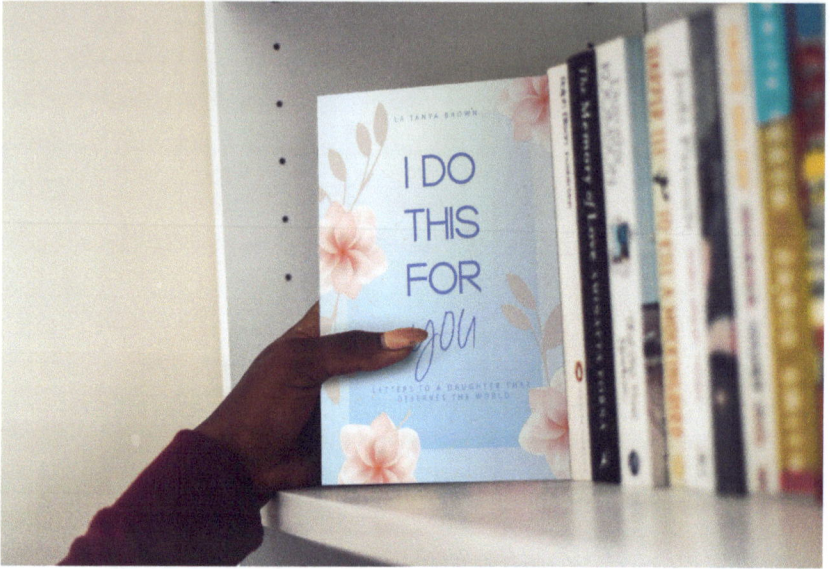

I wrote this book to mark down my love for my baby girl. I wanted her to read this and understand how much she means to me. This book is something that she could hold on to for the rest of her life, and she could pick it up as a reminder of who she is and just how much she is loved - no matter what is going on in her world. But as the idea began to unfold, I realized that this book is bigger than just that. This book is also something that mother's could give to their daughter's as something they can read for words of affirmation. Daughters around the world could hold this book and feel the embrace of their mother just from reading the love I have for my daughter. So, this book is dedicated to the most amazing daughter in the world, La Tanya and dedicated to the most amazing daughters throughout the world. Loving Parents, embrace your children so they can always remember your love. Children, embrace your loving parents because everything they do - they do it just for you. And they love you more than you could ever imagine.

As you read this book, insert your child's name into the pages. At the end of the book, glue their picture in the provided section and give this to them as a reminder of your love for them.

Table Of Contents

I've **Always** Loved You

I remember the first day
I laid eyes on you.
God knew I needed you.

You are my miracle.

"Many are the plans in the mind of a man, but it
is the purpose of the Lord that will stand."
Proverbs 19:21

You've taught me to be grateful and to embrace every memory.

Every hug, every kiss and every smile is held close to my heart.

I've Loved

Watching You

Grow

Figuring out life isn't the easiest but you've somehow managed to live yours to the fullest.

I constantly ask God to protect you and guide your footsteps as you are learning how to navigate life.

"So do not fear, for I am with you; do not be dismayed, for I am your God. I will strengthen you and help you; I will uphold you with my righteous right hand." Isaiah 41:10

"May the God of hope fill you with all joy and peace in believing, so that by the power of the Holy Spirit you may abound in hope." Romans 15:13

Keep God first and pray for others -
no matter what. Life has a way of
throwing some curveballs at you every
now and then, but as you pray
through the good and the bad - God
will see you through.

"I would have lost heart, unless I had believed That I would see the goodness of the LORD In the land of the living."
Psalm 27:13

"Let us not become weary in doing good, for at the proper time, we will reap a harvest if we do not give up."
Galatians 6:9

You will surely see the goodness of God. Keep going. Don't give up. No matter what attacks come against you, God's word says that NO WEAPON formed against you will prosper.

The Bible doesn't say that the weapon will not form - but it says that it will not prosper. That means no matter what attack the devil tries to bring your way - you will always overcome it. You're a world changer, so I know that you will fight and conquer every battle that comes your way, and even during the times when you feel like you can't keep going, know that I will always be here for you.

I am so proud of who you are.

Choose To Be A Leader

"Do not follow the crowd in doing wrong..." Exodus 23:2

Always aim for the best - as you have always done. Never settle for less. The balance with this is not allowing people to define your limits. Create boundaries. In life, your peers and/or coworkers will try to push you beyond your limits - and it's okay to say no. But there's also going to be people that may want you to settle - and it will be up to you to keep the bar high without settling for less than you know you are capable of achieving.

"Do not be deceived: "Bad company ruins good morals."

1 Corinthians 15:33

Know that I will always be here for you, but there's going to be times where I won't be around - and you must decide to do what is best for you. There are going to be times where you have to decide to lead instead of follow. Decide to keep good company. Your network influences your decisions. I'm always going to tell you to do life with God and allow Him to lead you - but your decisions are always going to be up to you. Let your decisions be founded upon honorable values, His Word and the feeling in your heart that tells you "yes" or "no" - that's the Holy Spirit. He will help you in all seasons and all decisions of your life.

"No temptation has overtaken you that is not common to man. God is faithful, and he will not let you be tempted beyond your ability, but with the temptation he will also provide the way of escape, that you may be able to endure it." 1 Corinthians 10:13

"But the Helper, the Holy Spirit, whom the Father will send in My name, He will teach you all things, and bring to your remembrance all things that I said to you." John 14:26

You Can Always Talk To Me

As a parent, I always want to make sure that my children can come to me with anything. I never want you to feel ashamed or fearful to ask me for feedback / advice on things that are on your mind. I prefer you to come to me than to find out from someone who is giving advice without the heart of wisdom.

You have grown beautifully into YOU

Teens may go through puberty stages and the pressure to try to enhance their beauty, but baby girl - you are beautiful already. Your confidence shouldn't come from someone else - it begins with how you feel about yourself. As your mom, I will always be your biggest cheerleader and I will always see you as the brightest star in the sky; but I want you to always remember that you truly are beautiful and no one can take that away from you.

_____, I want to let you know that I am extremely proud of you. You are growing up into a beautiful, successful young lady. I've watched you grow, and you've made your mother beyond proud. My praises can last forever, but the reality is - life happens, and there will be many times in life where it will feel as though life is not okay. As you are journeying your soon to be young adult life, I want to be the first one to give you advice and wisdom on what being an adult is really about. Here, you're going to read important things to remember regarding being a lady, handling mental health and encouragement when you transition into 17 and beyond.

Independence

A lot of young people look forward to growing up, fast. They try to keep up with the social media influencers while also racing to remain relevant in their friend's groups. What I've learned about life is to enjoy one day at a time. Growing up does bring independence, but independence means responsibility. Independence isn't all about doing what you want to do. Yes, you will be able to make your own decisions, but the weight of independence is being accountable for those very decisions that you make.

Independence is also more than moving into your own place, it is about establishing your own convictions, values, defining who YOU are and what you will be in life. That's the beautiful thing about independence. "Freedom" is vague. True freedom is defining your best life on terms that are founded upon the truth of God's word, the truth of who He created you to be and the truth of what you believe is best for your life. When you combine those three factors, you will feel the freedom that so many are searching for, but are so far away from. I have always instilled in you to keep God FIRST, and everything else shall follow. Keep God first in your decisions, your friendships and most of all your journey. As you spread your wings and fly into womanhood, surrender your independence to the Lord's direction and you will never fail.

"In all your ways know and acknowledge and recognize Him, And He will make your paths straight and smooth [removing obstacles that block your way]."
Proverbs 3:6
Amplified Version

Managing The Stress of Life

You truly have the strength of a superhero, but I want you to know that you aren't meant to carry the weight of the world. One thing about superheroes in the movies is that no one understands the weight of their responsibility. No one ever thinks to dig into the heart of the hero - they abandon themselves to save everyone. As you are growing up, I want you to know that it is not your responsibility to carry the weight of the world. No one was born to do this, except one person - and that was Jesus. But even Jesus asked if it was God's will that the burden be lifted from Him in Matthew 26:39 - **but He understood His assignment**. Jesus was born to take on the sin of the world - and only He was worthy and capable of doing that. You can't do everything, your arms aren't made to take on all the weights of the world.

You can't fix EVERYTHING.

Knowing that you have the heart of a hero, I have to remind you of this, so you don't destroy yourself. When a hero takes on too much pressure, they find themselves in a vulnerable situation that causes them to lose control. People have a way of wanting to take, take and take. But it is our responsibility to have the strength to say no, in order to protect our mental health. We have to give God our weights and leave it to Him to hold - which means leave it there and don't pick it back up.

"Give your burdens to the LORD, and he will take care of you. He will not permit the godly to slip and fall."
Psalm 55:22 (NLT)

Stress will come and go, but know that you can and will overcome it. The only thing capable of keeping you from being all that God has made you to be, is you. Don't get in your own way. Know when to go, know when to rest. Know when to say no, know when to say yes.

I also want you to know that the Lord will keep you in times of trouble. No matter what, keep pursuing Christ. In those times of darkness when depression tries to creep in - pursue God and stand on the truth. Yes, the fight will come, but God's truth is stronger than any circumstance or devil that tries to come against you. Your faith will keep you in times of trouble.

"Therefore my brethren, be ye steadfast, unmovable always abounding in the work of the Lord, forasmuch as ye know that your labour is not in vain in the Lord"

I Corinthians 15:58

I pray for you constantly, and it is a blessing to see God answer my prayers, even when it seems overwhelming.

If you ever find yourself at rock bottom, you will discover that He was always there for you.

Continue to hold on to His Word, His presence and His love - these are the only things that will remain.

"Give all your worries and cares to God,
for he cares about you."
1 Peter 5:7 (NLT)

Friends, Distractions & Acquaintances

When I was a child, I spoke as a child, I understood as a child. I thought as a child: but when I became an adult. I put away childish things. 1 Corinthians 14:11

Now that you're reaching this new adulthood. You are going to find out a lot about friendships vs associates, loyalty vs dishonesty. And being that you have the heart of a hero, and loyal as a true companion, you may feel the need to rescue your friends and save them from everything. One thing you will learn about as you are growing up with new people in your life is that you can't save people that don't want to be helped. This is hard to hear and accept when you are someone that has a big heart. Have you ever heard the instructions of a lifeguard trying to save someone that is drowning? They instruct the drowning individual not to panic. If they both panic, they will both go down.

As someone who wants to save the world, imagine how this can affect them when someone is drowning that doesn't really want the help. There are many people in the world that only think and care about their own good. They will seek out your help as they drown and ultimately drag you down with them. These types of people will take what they can from you but will only appear and attempt to take advantage of you in your times of vulnerability. You always have to protect/guard yourself from those types of people. The destruction may come in the form of peer pressure, it may even come as an ultimatum. Whatever it is, you will feel the absence of peace - and that is God warning you to get out of that situation.

"Do not be conformed to this world, but be transformed by the renewal of your mind, that by testing you may discern what is the will of God, what is good and acceptable and perfect." Romans 12:2 (ESV)

_____, you have too much to offer or give to ever let anyone take advantage of you. You are special with only the world to gain;

keep your eyes open and pray for God's protection from these individuals that will try to come into your space. Understand that everyone is NOT there for your best interest. EVERYONE DOES NOT HAVE GOOD INTENTIONS. As a child, we look at life with a naivety that is innocent and pure - but that is not reality. Now that you are growing up, I want you to seek God for discernment. Ask Him to show you who is in your life that is a friend, a distraction or a seasonal acquaintance. And when He does show you, believe Him. This way you can create healthy boundaries for your life, expectations and also protect your heart.

Always Remember

I am So Proud Of You

I know that you are always striving for the best and running toward success at full speed. Outside of the success and outside of your many accomplishments baby girl, I want you to know that I am truly proud of you. You don't ask for much, but I want to give you the world. Not because you've earned it, but because I feel that you deserve it.

I Never Meant To Hurt You

Thank you for trusting me to be your mom during the hard times. I ask you to forgive me if you've ever felt neglected, unsafe, unloved or too sheltered. I never meant to hurt you if I have.

You Are My Best Friend

I love talking to you and spending time with you. I want you to know that I truly consider you my best friend. Yes, I know, I'm your mom, but I see you as the last puzzle piece to the finished puzzle. People don't think I break, but I do. You have managed to help me keep the broken pieces of me together - from the love that you give me. Thank you for respecting me even when others haven't. I know it's hard seeing me hurt and in pain, but I thank you for loving me through it all. Don't let my pain determine your future. God has a plan for your life and I will be here to help as much as I can.

You Are Brilliant

You are such a unique and special girl. God truly
spent quality time creating you. I've never met
someone so down to earth, humble and kind as
you. Your success doesn't define you - who you
are is enough. God MADE YOU BRILLIANT.
Everything about you is special. You don't have
to depend on success to validate you. God
validated you before you were born.

You Are Worthy Of Love

Never settle, baby. You are worthy of love. You don't have to rush into relationships and you don't have to ever settle for being tolerated. You have a beautiful heart and it deserves to be taken care of by someone that truly deserves you. Think of yourself as a priceless piece of art. You should not be mishandled, mistreated and/or disrespected. You deserve the best when it comes to love, and even being loved by friends. Don't settle, only accept the best of the best.

Keep Your Peace

Don't let anyone steal your shine. God created you as a Radiant person. If someone or something is stealing your joy - cut it. Your peace of mind is the best thing you can have besides Jesus. When it comes to jobs, decisions and people - keep your peace. Money, recognition and acceptance isn't worth it if your peace is at stake. It's okay to not be okay. Get help when you need it. Communicate with a professional and you can also come to me. I'm here for you even when you're not okay because you'll always be my daughter

Everything I Do
Is For You.

I Love You,

Mommy

You Will Always Be My Baby Girl

[Paste Your Child's Photo Here]

www.ingramcontent.com/pod-product-compliance
Lightning Source LLC
Chambersburg PA
CBHW040036110426
42741CB00031B/113